About this

Over the last forty
a multibillion-dolla
are everywhere an   ~ popularization
of video games has ..... a growing concern about their ability to transform
those who play them into antisocial killing machines who are desensitized to
violence, have no friends, and will forever live in their parents' basements. But
are these fears based in reality?

Over the last twenty years, psychologists, sociologists, and media scholars have
been working hard to answer these questions. Until now, their findings have
largely remained insulated within scientific circles and inaccessible to the general
public. A Parent's Guide to Video Games breaks the long-standing barriers
between science and society by providing the first comprehensive guide to the
science behind the headlines.

Drawing from the most recent research in the field of game studies, A Parent's
Guide to Video Games was developed specifically to help parents better
understand if, how, and why video game play can impact a child's physical, social,
and psychological well-being. This includes addressing questions such as these:

*Will playing violent video games make my child more aggressive
and more likely to commit violent crime?*

*Is video game addiction real? If so, how do I know if my child is
addicted to video games?*

*Will video game play worsen the symptoms of attention deficit
disorder (ADD)?*

Answers to these questions and many more are discussed inside. Armed with
accurate and up-to-date scientific information, parents will begin to understand
the science behind the headlines and be able to make more informed decisions
for themselves and their families.

About the author

Dr. Rachel Kowert is a research psychologist from Austin, Texas,
with a PhD in psychology from the University of York (UK) and
an MA in counseling psychology from Santa Clara University. Dr.
Kowert has dedicated her career to studying video games and the
gamers who love them. As a researcher, psychologist, gamer, and
parent, she strives to educate other parents about the potential dangers and
unique contributions that video games can bring to our everyday lives.

"Dr. Rachel Kowert explores once again the possibility of a connection between some hot-topic psychological disorders like attention deficit disorder and video games. All parents around the world should examine Kowert's lucid guide regarding violence, sexism, and social concerns with video game players. Using factual data, Dr. Kowert draws conclusions to which of these disorders can scientifically be linked to video games, and determines others that are just hearsay. Alternatively, Kowert also cites many links in which video games may enhance cognitive development and intellectual skills. A Parent's Guide to Video Games is a must for all mothers and fathers to understand the impact video games might have on their children, and how to wield them to improve your child's development."

Chris Chandler and **Dean McCarthy** of GamingWithSwag.com

"This is a concise, wonderfully helpful resource for parents who are nervous -- or just curious -- about psychological research on the effects of video games, and who might otherwise fall down a rabbit-hole of misinformation and scaremongering on a frequently misunderstood subject."

Jesse Singal
Writer-at-large, New York Magazine

"Many parents worry that if they buy their child the latest video game, that this may cause the youth harm. Parents have to sift through considerable alarmism, fear-mongering and deceptive reporting of research to get through the truth. Finally, with Rachel Kowert's book, A Parent's Guide to Video Games, parents have it all lain out in front of them. Dr. Kowert covers up-to-date research in language easily digestible by non-scientists. Sometimes what games do or do not do defies simply "yes/no" answers, but Dr. Kowert provides the information parents need to make informed and individual decisions that will be right for their families. I highly recommend it for all parents."

Dr. Christopher Ferguson
Professor of Psychology at Stetson University

"How can parents tell if their kid's video game play is normal or potentially unhealthy? A Parent's Guide to Video Games is an excellent resource written by a scientist who has spent her career exploring video games and their effects on society. Rather than providing a simple, headline-grabbing treatment of the potential negatives of video games, Dr. Kowert summarizes the most recent research in a way parents can understand and provides common-sense suggestions that can help parents make the most of their children's video game play. Her balanced approach will help parents interpret the current debates about video games and give them the tools they need to promote healthy game play."

Dr. Michelle Colder Carras
Postdoctoral Research Fellow in Public Mental Health

A Parent's Guide to Video Games

The essential guide to understanding how video games impact your child's physical, social, and psychological well-being

Dr. Rachel Kowert

Design and Illustration by Jim Trippier

ISBN: 1537359835
ISBN 13: 9781537359830
Library of Congress Control Number: 2016915621
CreateSpace Independent Publishing Platform, North Charleston, SC

*This book is dedicated to the faculty of
the Education and Counseling Psychology
department at Santa Clara University. Thank you
for showing me that the most valuable endeavors
are those done in the service of others.*

Contents

An Introduction to Video Game Research

First it was the radio. Then it was film, television, rock and roll, and comic books. Today, video games have become the scapegoat of choice for a variety of societal problems, including gun violence, obesity, and addictive behaviors. The fears surrounding the potential negative influence of video games have become more exaggerated and widespread as they have become more popular, more realistic in design, and now, as they are networked online.

Video gaming is a multibillion-dollar industry supported by a community of over a billion players worldwide[1,2]. However, the unprecedented growth of the video game industry has increased concern about the impact that video games may have on players' physical, social, and psychological well-being. This is particularly the case when discussing violent video games. Turn on the news at any given hour, especially after a violent tragedy perpetrated by a young male, and you are likely to catch a glimpse of these fears. From the Columbine High School shootings of 1999[3] to the more recent shootings in Aurora, Colorado[4] and Newtown, Connecticut[5], the news media consistently claims that these incidents are at least partially motivated by violent video games.

> THE GROWTH OF THE VIDEO GAME INDUSTRY HAS INCREASED CONCERN ABOUT THE IMPACT THAT VIDEO GAMES MAY HAVE.

Contrary to earlier media-based fears, the panic surrounding video games largely stems from their interactivity. That is, unlike watching television or film where the story continues with or without you, video games require the player to interact with them via a keyboard, game controller, or smartphone screen. Thus, rather than watching Sylvester Stallone kill

> THE PANIC SURROUNDING VIDEO GAMES LARGELY STEMS FROM THEIR INTERACTIVITY.

enemies on a battlefield in the film *Rambo*, in the game, you are *Rambo*, and you are killing enemies on a battlefield. This difference is key and is part of the reason video games are believed to have a more powerful influence on those who play them than other forms of media.

Violence is not the only concern, however, as video games are also thought to aggravate the symptoms of attention deficit disorder (ADD), depression, and obesity, as well as cultivate sexist and misogynistic behavior. Parents are also increasingly concerned that their children's love for video games may turn into addiction, as they begin to fall behind on schoolwork or fail to meet their commitments. New concerns related to online games have also developed over the last few years—including the rising concern that online gaming friends may be replacing "real-world" friends, which may lead to the loss of peer friendships and, consequently, isolation.

> PARENTS ARE INCREASINGLY CONCERNED THAT THEIR CHILDREN'S LOVE FOR VIDEO GAMES MAY TURN INTO ADDICTION.

Perhaps unsurprisingly, the parents of children and adolescents are those who most often express worry about video game effects. This is partially because children and adolescents undergo several important developmental stages where peer-to-peer interaction is critical, such as the development

TIME SPENT PLAYING VIDEO GAMES WITH FRIENDS AFTER SCHOOL IS NOT NECESSARILY SOMETHING FOR PARENTS TO WORRY ABOUT.

of social and emotional skills[6]. Generally speaking, time spent playing video games with friends after school is not necessarily something for parents to worry about. However, vast amounts of time spent playing video games alone or online could be cause for concern, as these activities inevitability take time away from face-to-face activities. Additionally, because of the rapid development children and adolescents undergo, they are believed to be more vulnerable to the influence of video games, particularly in relation to violent or sexualized content[7,8].

On the following pages, the science behind the claims of video game effects will be unpacked, explored, and examined, with a special focus on the possible impact on children and adolescent players. The hope is that this information will bring clarity to the debates about the effects of video games that have dominated our popular culture over the last forty years. With this knowledge, parents can be empowered to make more informed decisions for themselves and their families.

115 million

Americans play video games that is 36% of the population of the United States!

4 out of 5

US households own a device to play videogames.

90%

of university students report having played video games[8]

55% of males play
44% of females play

$23.5 billion

spent on video games in 2015

The above information comes from the annual report of the Entertainment Software Association (2016)[1].

1

Addiction

People who play video games frequently are often said to be addicted to them. We should be careful, however, to reserve the "video game addiction" buzzword for the actions of those individuals who truly display the signs of behavioral addiction to video games. Over the last decade, a wealth of research has aided psychologists in better understanding what video game addiction is, what the keys are to identifying it, and what we should do if our children or someone we know shows early warning signs.

? What is video game addiction?

The American Psychiatric Association (APA) refers to video game addiction as "Internet Gaming Disorder." It does not, at this point, officially recognize it as a behavioral addiction, because it is not formally cataloged in the official Diagnostic and Statistical Manual of Mental Disorders (DSM)[9]. However, the APA has identified Internet Gaming Disorder as a topic that requires additional research to determine if it should be included in the next edition of the DSM. This call to action has prompted a wealth of research in the area and has led to great strides in better understanding the signs, symptoms, and potential treatment plans for gaming addiction.

> **GAMING ADDICTION IS NOT PRESENT UNTIL PLAYERS HAVE LOST CONTROL OVER THEIR PLAYING.**

ⓘ It is noteworthy that Internet Gaming Disorder has been identified as a topic of interest by the APA before other potential behavioural disorders such as sex addiction or work addiction (workaholism).

Several models of video game addiction have been developed. Drawing from previous models of addictive behavior, these models have all been built on the distinction that it is only an addictive behavior if the person has "a persistent and uncontrollable urge to consume a substance or engage in an activity that results in significant personal harm and interpersonal conflict for the user[10,11]." Thus, gaming addiction is not present until players have lost control over their playing and it has begun to have a detrimental effect on all aspects of their lives, including education, work, friendships, hobbies, general health, and psychological well-being[10,11].

Rates of addiction and problematic video game play are generally low, typically reported to be less than 10 percent of the general video game

RATES OF ADDICTION AND PROBLEMATIC VIDEO GAME PLAY ARE GENERALLY LOW.

playing population[11,12]. However, the rates may be far lower than that, as a recent study found that only 0.2 percent of game players assessed met all of the criteria for gaming addiction, as outlined below[13].

❓ What are the signs of video game addiction?

To determine if a person is addicted to video games, several criteria must be met. The most basic of these is a persistent and uncontrollable urge to play video games that results in significant personal harm or other personal consequences in all aspects of their life, including job/educational activities, personal relationships, hobbies, and physical and mental health[10]. Dr. Mark Griffiths, a chartered psychologist and video game addiction expert has proposed a detailed, six-component model of gaming addiction[14]. In this model, an addiction to video games is apparent if players meet and sustain the following criteria for a period of three to six months. If these patterns remain for a shorter period of time, they may simply indicate a temporary fixation on video games. These criteria include[11]:

 Salience: Video game play begins to dominate the player's thoughts, emotions, and behavior. Video games become the most important activity in the player's life. He or she becomes preoccupied with playing and, when not playing, is planning the next play session. Normal activities are abandoned as the person succumbs to the addictive craving for game play.

 Mood Modification: The player experiences a change in mood because of video game play. This can include feelings of euphoria, tranquility, or relaxation, as well as changes in physiological patterns when playing, such as increased heart rate.

✔ **Conflict:** The player begins to suffer negative interpersonal, occupational, psychological, and extracurricular consequences due to excessive gaming. These can include conflict with family and friends, the loss of a job or failure in school, a withdrawal from participation in other activities, and psychological distress, such as increased depression.

✔ **Tolerance:** The player needs ever increasing amounts of play time to achieve the mood-modifying effects. As such, play time continues to increase over time.

✔ **Withdrawal:** When players are unable to play, they become frustrated and irritable. To avoid these negative feelings, players will try to minimize the time spent between play sessions.

✔ **Relapse:** As with other addictions, players may repeatedly fail to reduce their video game use. Continued relapse indicates further loss of control over behavior, which is a key component of addiction.

While a checklist approach to identifying video game addiction like the one outlined above has been widely adopted by researchers and clinicians, it is just one of many kinds of approaches that have been proposed[15,16]. As a relatively new field of study, it will be some time before a standardized assessment for diagnosing Internet Gaming Disorder is implemented.

❓ How do I know if my child is addicted to video games?

If your child meets all of the criteria mentioned above for a sustained period of at least three months, he or she may be showing signs of gaming addiction, and further action may need to be taken. However, keep in mind that high engagement is often confused with addiction. If your child is displaying signs associated with the criteria outlined above for less than three months, then he or she may simply be highly engaged[17] or temporarily fixated, and

RATES OF ADDICTION AND PROBLEMATIC VIDEO GAME PLAY ARE GENERALLY LOW.

not showing signs of addiction. Remember that an addiction is present only when video game play causes significant personal consequences over a sustained time period, usually of more than three months.

It is worth noting that some groups of players have been found to be more vulnerable to video game addiction than others. Specifically, problematic game play and addictive behavior have been found to be more common among males[12] and players who show the symptoms of attention-deficit hyperactivity disorder (ADHD)[18]. The reasons for higher rates of problematic and addictive behavior among these groups are unclear. It should also be pointed out that many researchers believe video game addiction can occur with both offline and online video game playing, despite the distinction made by the APA for recommending more research evaluating gaming addiction among online games in particular (i.e., Internet Gaming Disorder).

HIGH ENGAGEMENT IS OFTEN CONFUSED WITH ADDICTION.

 ## Take Home Message

"Video game addiction" and "high video game engagement" are terms that are often mistaken as interchangeable. Frequent video game play may transition into addictive behavior when the player begins to experience significant personal consequences due to play and demonstrates signs of salience, mood modification, conflict, tolerance, withdrawal, and relapse for more than a three-month period.

 Advice to parents

Video games are now ever-present in the lives of our children and adolescents, and it can be hard to draw the line as to how much is too much. Unfortunately, there is no magic number. The best advice I can give is to be mindful of any behavior changes in your children relating to the warning signs outlined above. If your child or someone you know continues to play video games despite a range of negative life consequences due to their play, they may potentially be showing signs of addiction. Seek help from a mental health professional if you believe your child is showing signs of significant interpersonal, occupational, and/or psychological consequences because of video game play. While specific treatment programs for problematic and addictive gaming are relatively limited, cognitive-behavioral therapy has shown promise in small, well-controlled studies[11]. It is also important to keep in mind that excessive or problematic game play could be a symptom or coping mechanism for a number of other underlying issues, such as depression, social anxiety, or substance abuse.

BE MINDFUL OF ANY BEHAVIOR CHANGES IN YOUR CHILDREN.

2

Aggression and Violent Crime

The possibility that violent video game play will desensitize players to real-world violence, increase aggression, and incite violent tendencies is a top concern for parents. But what does the research say? Do violent video games desensitize players to real-world violence and turn them into "killing machines"?

? What is a violent video game?

Violent video games include elements of violent action that are actively committed by the player or by other individuals (such as online players or nonplayable characters) and witnessed by the player. Violent actions include fighting, using weapons, and aggressive or inciting language.

VIOLENT ELEMENTS CAN BE FOUND IN MANY GAMES ACROSS GENRE CATEGORIES.

Violent content may or may not be realistic in terms of appearance (graphics) or content (fighting in a fantasy world). While violence may be the defining feature of many popular video game franchises, violent elements can be found in many games across genre categories (for example, role playing, action adventure, and party games, among others).

? Will playing violent video games make my child more aggressive?

Hundreds of scientific studies have evaluated the relationship between violent video game play and aggression. Of these, many have reported small, short-term increases in aggression following exposure to violent video games[20-25]. While this may seem like a reason to sound the alarm, it is important to note that these increases in aggression are typically measured within the first few minutes following violent video game play, and there has been no evidence to suggest that these short-term rises have any long-term impact on players' level of aggression[26–28].

THERE IS NO EVIDENCE TO SUGGEST THAT SHORT-TERM RISES IN AGGRESSION HAVE ANY LONG-TERM IMPACT ON PLAYERS.

In fact, many research studies have concluded that there are no significant links between violent video game play and aggression[24,26,29,30] or other undesirable behavioral outcomes such as antisocial attitudes or bullying behavior among children and adolescents[29].

It is important to point out that many scientific studies that claim to have found links between violent video games and aggression have been criticized for the ways in which the aggression was measured[24,31]. For example, one widely used measure of aggression asks research participants to finish a word completion task following violent video game play. The task typically consists of

MANY STUDIES HAVE CONCLUDED THAT THERE ARE NO SIGNIFICANT LINKS BETWEEN VIOLENT VIDEO GAME PLAY AND AGGRESSION.

a series of words with letters missing, and players must complete the words in a short amount of time with the first word they can think of to fill in the blanks. Depending on the letters people choose, different words can be formed.

eg Participants could be presented with the letters **K I _ _**. If players choose to complete the word by writing **K-I-L-L** rather than **K-I-S-S**, then their response would be considered representative of postgame play aggression[32,33].

Another popular method asks participants, immediately after playing a violent video game, to indicate how much hot sauce at what level of spiciness another research participant should be given to eat. Referred to as the "hot sauce paradigm"[34], a greater amount of hot sauce at a higher level of spiciness is thought to indicate greater aggression. It is difficult to see how being deemed more aggressive from these tests translate into real-world aggressive thoughts and behaviors.

? Will playing violent video games make my child more likely to commit violent crime?

While violent video game play has been linked to small, short-term increases in aggression, no relationship between violent video game play and violent behavior has been found. In fact, a direct relationship between violent video game play and violent behavior is highly unlikely. If there were a direct relationship, then we should have seen an increase in crime over the last twenty years that corresponded with the rise in the popularity of violent video games. Youth crime should have shown a particularly steep increase, since, presumably, teenagers have more time to dedicate to video game play (and thus, a greater exposure to the violent content), and they are more easily influenced by media messages than adults[7,8]. However, this increase has not occurred.

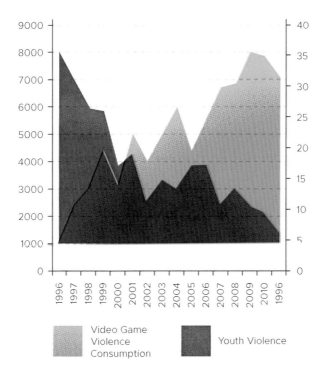

Societal Videogame Violence Consumption and Societal Youth Violence, 1996–2011 (reprinted with permission from Taylor & Francis)[21]

In fact, the opposite has been found as violent video game consumption has increased over the last twenty years alongside a steady decline in youth violence[21, 23]. As the relationship between these two variables is correlational (they are related but not in a cause-and-effect way), these findings do not mean that playing violent video games contributes to declines in real-world violence. Rather, the findings indicate the unlikelihood that violent video game play actively contributes to an increase in youth violence.

A DIRECT RELATIONSHIP BETWEEN VIOLENT VIDEO GAME PLAY AND VIOLENT BEHAVIOR IS HIGHLY UNLIKELY.

"Following violent tragedies involving young men, many frequently point to violent video games as a cause for the behavior, but the research does not back this up. As violent video games become more popular, it was understandable for them to fall under intense scrutiny, and claims about their harms and benefits may have been exaggerated, including by the scientific community"

Chistopher J. Ferguson
Professor of Psychology at Stetson University

Furthermore, other research in this area has found gender, previous exposure to violence, trait aggression (the level of aggressiveness innately held in one's personality), and the delinquency level of one's peers to be far more influential in determining if someone will commit a violent crime than exposure to violent media, including video games[23].

Will violent video games desensitize my child to violence?

There is an increasing amount of evidence to suggest that playing violent video games does not desensitize players to real-world violence[35,36]. Because our brains are great at differentiating between real-world violence and fictional violence, it is uncommon for people to generalize what they see and learn from fictional

OUR BRAINS ARE GREAT AT DIFFERENTIATING BETWEEN REAL-WORLD VIOLENCE AND FICTIONAL VIOLENCE.

contexts, such as shooting people in a video game, to real-world contexts, such as committing gun violence[35,37,38].

If you take a minute to recall how you feel when you watch a particularly violent movie and then compare that to how you think you would feel if you were to see the same violence occur right in front of you, you can get an idea of how our brains distinguish between the two. I am sure you would experience these two scenarios very differently!

 ## Take Home Message

In laboratory settings, small but significant short-term increases in aggression have been found after exposure to violent video game play. However, a lack of long-term effects suggests that the links between violent video game play and aggression are exaggerated. Research also indicates the unlikelihood of a direct relationship between violent video game play and violent behavior as youth crime has steadily declined alongside the rise in popularity of violent video games over the last twenty years. Fears of desensitization to real-world violence are also unsupported in the scientific literature, as our brains are great at differentiating between what is real and what is fictional. There is little chance of what we see and experience in one context being generalized to the other.

THERE IS LITTLE CHANCE OF WHAT WE SEE AND EXPERIENCE IN ONE CONTEXT BEING GENERALIZED TO THE OTHER.

Advice For Parents

While the fear that violent video game play is breeding a new generation of aggressive and violent children is largely unsupported by scientific research, violent video games are still not appropriate for players of all ages. Be sure to remain mindful of what your children are playing by checking the age ratings and content labels on the games that they play. While *Grand Theft Auto* (Take-Two Interactive) may not turn children into criminals, it will expose them to mature themes and actions not suitable for children under the age of seventeen (as suggested by its M age rating).

> **REMAIN MINDFUL OF WHAT YOUR CHILDREN ARE PLAYING BY CHECKING THE AGE RATINGS AND CONTENT LABELS.**

3

Cognitive Development

F or the last few years, there has been a growing concern about the impact of video games on intellectual development. While the basis of these concerns is unclear (perhaps it is because video games are associated with physical laziness?), the scientific research in this area has not found indicators of intellectual laziness among video game players. In fact, video game play has been found to help meet a wide range of needs related to the cognitive and intellectual development of children and adolescents[10].

? What is cognitive development?

Cognitive development (also known as intellectual development) refers to the development of various reasoning skills that we use to make sense of the world around us. This includes processes such as short- and long-term memory, information processing, logic, problem solving, and decision-making. The successful development of cognitive skills is important for general intelligence (as measured by standardized intelligence tests), as well as a range of other, more complex abilities, such as language development and perspective taking. While cognitive development continues through adulthood, it grows most rapidly through childhood and adolescence[40].

THE SUCCESSFUL DEVELOPMENT OF COGNITIVE SKILLS IS IMPORTANT FOR GENERAL INTELLIGENCE.

? Can cognitive skills be honed through video game play? If so, which ones?

Video game play has been associated with the improvement of a range of cognitive skills[39,41], such as improved goal setting, initiative taking, and persistence in the face of difficult challenges[39,42]. Video games are great vehicles for sharpening cognitive skills because they provide a wide range of different challenges within a single space. For example, in many games, players explore new spaces, solve puzzles, craft objects, and cooperate or compete with other players to achieve increasingly difficult tasks. These experiences are great for learning, as players must constantly develop new strategies and solutions for new problems in a relatively short amount of time.

Many video games also allow players to experiment with and adopt new identities through role-playing and pretend play. An old man can be young again, a woman can lead groups through the guise of a man, and anyone can be a strong warrior, mystical wizard or a caring healer. In addition to being fun, role-playing is important for the cognitive development of children and teenagers. It has been shown to aid in the successful development of a range of cognitive skills, including perspective taking, emotion regulation, and abstract thinking[43,44].

> *"You know what's really exciting about video games is you don't just interact with the game physically – you're not just moving your hand on a joystick, but you're asked to interact with the game psychologically and emotionally as well. You're not just watching the characters on the screen; you're becoming those characters"*

Nina Huntemann
Game Over

Perhaps most notably, video game play has been associated with improved visual information processing, often referred to as visual-spatial skills[41,45]. Visual-spatial skills, a cornerstone of many measures of intelligence, include abilities such as visual perception, visual processing, visual memory, and mental rotation.

ROLE-PLAYING IS IMPORTANT FOR THE COGNITIVE DEVELOPMENT OF CHILDREN AND TEENAGERS.

By challenging players to notice small changes in their environment and react quickly (as is often necessary in many action and action-adventure games), players hone their visual processing speed and accuracy. Researchers have also found that the transfer of visual-spatial skills from video games to real-world scenarios occurs easily[46].

TRY TO CHOOSE VIDEO GAMES FOR YOUR CHILDREN THAT ENCOURAGE PROBLEM SOLVING OR TEAMWORK.

It is important to note that there has been a lingering concern from many parents that aggressive competition in violent video games counteracts any potential positive

effects and, instead, promotes antisocial and aggressive behavior. However, there is no scientific evidence to suggest that violent video game play has long-term effects on cognitive or intellectual development[24].

Take Home Message

Video game play can help develop and hone a range of top cognitive and intellectual skills, including frustration tolerance, identity experimentation, leadership, teamwork, initiative taking, goal setting, and persistence. While it has been suggested that violent video game content interferes with learning by promoting antisocial or aggressive behavior, these claims are not supported by recent research. In fact, action and action-adventure games with violent content are often the very games that have been found to promote the development of a range of visual-spatial skills.

Advice For Parents

Games can be great learning tools to develop a range of cognitive and intellectual skills. To encourage cognitive development, try to choose video games for your children that encourage problem solving or teamwork. Action and action-adventure games are also great choices for developing a range of visual-spatial skills. Just keep in mind that online games that allow players to work in teams and some action-adventure games may not be appropriate for young children. Be sure to check the ratings and content descriptions for each game to determine which ones are appropriate for your child.

4

Physical and Mental Health

C oncerns about the impact video games have on children's physical and mental health are wide ranging. For example, there have been numerous claims that video game play promotes unhealthy sedentary lifestyles and aggrevates various mental health problems. While some of these claims may not be far from reality (for instance, playing video games can be a relatively sedentary activity), the research findings in this area are far from black and white.

What does the research say about video game play and obesity?

As a culture, Americans live a relatively sedentary lifestyle[47]. We drive to school or work instead of walk or bicycle. We sit at our desks for at least eight hours a day, and then we go home to enjoy relatively sedentary leisure activities, such as watching television, going to the movies, and playing video games. As a general rule, leading an inactive life is unhealthy. As such, if video games are a person's only leisure activity, then it could be argued that playing video games contributes to a range of physical consequences associated with inactivity, including obesity.

That being said, if a person is suffering from obesity, it is unlikely that playing video games was the only activity that contributed to that condition. In fact, video game players have been found to be no more or less overweight than those who do not play video games[48,49].

In a 2008 research study, online game players were found to have an average body mass index (BMI; a standard measure of fitness) of **25.19**. While this is considered to be slightly overweight, it is substantially lower than **28**, which was the BMI of an average American adult at the time[48].

Recent developments in improved video- and controller-tracking technology opened the door to a range of new games that get players moving. Such games, dubbed "exergames," take advantage of motion-tracking technologies through innovative control design, such as motion-sensing cameras. The rise of exergames may deserve some of the credit for keeping game

AS A GENERAL RULE, LEADING AN INACTIVE LIFE IS UNHEALTHY.

players fit. Some popular examples include *Just Dance* (Ubisoft), which guides players through fast-paced dance routines to popular songs, and *Wii Fit* (Nintendo), which guides players through a series of exercises to improve balance and strength[49]. While the research has not yet demonstrated that playing exergames directly contributes to weight loss[50], players have been found to expend over 50 percent more energy than if they were playing a traditional, sedentary video game[51].

THE RISE OF EXERGAMES MAY DESERVE SOME OF THE CREDIT FOR KEEPING GAME PLAYERS FIT.

 So-called augmented reality games that use geolocation, such as *Pokémon GO* (Niantic), are also being widely lauded for getting gamers moving[52]. These games engage with the local environment by requiring players to go outside and find objects or solve puzzles. They also often encourage working together with others players nearby.

AUGMENTED REALITY GAMES ARE BEING WIDELY LAUDED FOR GETTING GAMERS MOVING.

These games are not without their own danger, however, as several players of *Pokémon GO* have injured themselves by not paying attention to their surroundings[53]. If your children show interest in these games, make sure you remind them to keep a close eye on what is going on around them—and to not drive while playing *Pokémon*.

Will video game play worsen the symptoms of ADD?

Children with ADD, either with or without a hyperactivity component, typically struggle to remain attentive and focused on a task. As video games are often fast paced, many have wondered whether prolonged play may aggravate the attention problems associated with ADD by reinforcing the pattern of short bursts of focused attention rather than sustained concentration.

Contrary to these claims, video games have emerged as promising tools to help improve attention and reduce impulsivity for individuals who show symptoms of ADD[29]. For example, a review of the research in 2014 revealed that children and adults who played action video games (e.g., games from the *Tomb Raider* [Square Enix] and *Fallout* [Interplay Entertainment] series) showed improved sustained attention and reduced impulsivity over time[54]. Training programs developed to reduce inattention and distractibility for children with ADD have also been found to be more successful when they incorporate game elements. As noted by the researchers, attention problems and distractibility associated with ADD seem to disappear when the child is concentrating on video games as compared to more traditional training programs[55]. This is at least partially because children with ADD have been found to perform better with novel, stimulating tasks that offer immediate rewards, which many video games provide[29].

VIDEO GAMES HAVE EMERGED AS PROMISING TOOLS TO HELP IMPROVE ATTENTION AND REDUCE IMPULSIVITY.

CHILDREN WITH ADD HAVE BEEN FOUND TO PERFORM BETTER WITH NOVEL, STIMULATING TASKS.

While this research is promising and indicates that video games may be a useful tool for helping improve attention and impulsivity for children and adolescents with ADD, more research is needed before video game play can be recommended as part of a treatment plan.

❓ What are the links between video game play, depression, and social anxiety?

Video games are stereotyped as an activity for those who are depressed and socially anxious[56]. Perhaps because children and teenagers often play video games alone, the concern that video game play can contribute to worsening symptoms of depression and social anxiety is growing among parents and researchers alike.

THERE IS NO EVIDENCE TO SUGGEST THAT DEPRESSION OR SOCIAL ANXIETY WORSENS DUE TO PLAYING VIDEO GAMES.

Partially supporting these concerns, researchers have found that people who play online games exhibit a higher rate of depression than the general US population[48]. Furthermore, those who play online games more frequently show higher rates of depression than those who play less frequently[57]. Similarly, heavier users of online games and players who display signs of video game addiction have shown higher levels of social anxiety than those who play less frequently or who do not show signs of video game addiction[58,59]. However, research has not yet determined

RESEARCHERS HAVE FOUND THAT PEOPLE WHO PLAY ONLINE GAMES EXHIBIT A HIGHER RATE OF DEPRESSION.

whether online games directly contribute to these outcomes or if people with depression and social anxiety are more likely to play online games. The latter seems more likely as there is no evidence to suggest that depression or social anxiety worsens over time due to playing video games, with the exception of players who show signs of problematic and/or addicted video game play. For this subgroup of players, depressive and anxious symptoms have been found to worsen over time, with the game play itself directly contributing to the problem[60,61].

> "A game is an opportunity to focus our energy, with relentless optimism, at something we're good at (or getting better at) and enjoy. In other words, gameplay is the direct emotional opposite of depression"

Jane McGonigal
Reality is Broken: Why Games Make Us Better and How They Can Change the World

Take Home Message

Video games have not been found to exacerbate the symptoms of ADD; in fact, they may actually help children and adolescents with ADD control their inattentiveness and distractibility. Direct links between video game play and obesity have also not been supported by the research. However, as video game play can be largely a sedentary activity (with the exceptions of exergames and augmented reality games like *Pokémon GO*), it should not be your child's only leisure activity, or it may begin to contribute to declines in physical health. Lastly, while online game play is often thought to exacerbate symptoms of

DIRECT LINKS BETWEEN VIDEO GAME PLAY AND OBESITY HAVE NOT BEEN SUPPORTED BY THE RESEARCH.

depression, research has not found this to be the case among the general game-playing population. However, research has found problematic and addictive video game play to be associated with elevated levels of depressive symptoms.

 **Advice For Parents**

Too much of anything is never good a thing. While video game play could hold the potential to improve sustained attention and reduce impulsivity among children with ADD, not enough research has been done in this area to conclude whether or not video game play should be integrated into treatment

USE YOUR CHILDREN'S VIDEO GAME INTERESTS AS A JUMPING OFF POINT FOR OTHER ACTIVITIES.

plans. If you want to encourage your children to try exergaming, find a game that offers fun, short-term challenges that adapt to their skill level. This will help keep motivation high. Games that have the option of being played together with friends are even better, as everything is more fun when done together. Don't be afraid to use your children's video game interests as a jumping off point for other activities. Do they like to play *NBA 2K17* (2K Games)? Then why not take them out to the courts for a friendly game?

5

Sexism and Misogyny

C oncerns over a potentially sexist and misogynistic gaming culture being cultivated online were brought into the mainstream in 2012, when Anita Sarkeesian became the victim of online harassment because of her Kickstarter campaign to produce a Tropes vs. Women in Video Games web series. Since then, many have wondered whether online gaming cultures are not only condoning sexism and misogynic behavior, but also cultivating these attitudes within gaming communities.

Why are video games thought to cultivate sexist attitudes, beliefs, and behaviors?

It is no secret that video game content is predominately male-oriented. There are few female lead characters in large franchises[62,63] and those franchises that that do feature female characters typically depict them in sexualized ways[64,65]. Lara Croft from the *Tomb Raider* series (Square Enix) would be an example of this trend.

It should be noted that significant efforts have been made over the last few years to transition Lara Croft away from her traditional over-sexualized appearance.

Most female characters, however, are secondary and tend to be placed in significantly unflattering roles within the story of the games. For instance, in the popular *Grand Theft Auto* video game series (Take-Two Interactive),

THERE ARE FEW FEMALE LEAD CHARACTERS IN LARGE FRANCHISES.

females are relegated to the roles of stripper, prostitute, or helpless victim[66].

 For more discussion on the roles women typically hold in video games, check out the aforementioned web series, *Tropes vs. Women in Video Games*[67], on YouTube, hosted by Anita Sarkeesian.

The problem is that constant and prolonged exposure to the underrepresentation and misrepresentation of women in video games is thought to cultivate sexist thoughts, attitudes, and behaviors among the mostly male video game players[68]. That is, the overwhelming portrayal of women in unflattering

MISREPRESENTATION OF WOMEN IN VIDEO GAMES IS THOUGHT TO CULTIVATE SEXIST ATTITUDES.

and stereotypical roles is believed to turn the interactive space[69] of a video game into a highly influential method of teaching prejudice against women, whether intentional or not. This concern grows in regard to teenage players, as they are at a greater risk for influence via media[7,8].

 Sexism; the exclusion of and discrimination toward an individual because of their gender.

Misogyny; dislike, contempt for, and ingrained prejudice against women because of their gender.

❓ Do video games cultivate sexism?

Researchers have found that male players who are exposed to stereotypical representations of women in video games report being more tolerant of sexual harassment[70], and they are more likely to agree with statements that women are weak and need a man's protection[71]. However, when following the same players over time, no evidence has been found to indicate that sexist beliefs become cultivated over time due to video game play alone[72]. Thus, there may

THERE MAY BE SOME SHORT-TERM CHANGES IN ATTITUDES AND BELIEFS FOLLOWING EXPOSURE TO SEXIST CONTENT.

be some short-term changes in attitudes and beliefs following exposure to sexist content in video games, but video game play does not seem to cultivate further sexist beliefs over time.

❓ Are online gaming cultures sexist and/or misogynistic?

While research has not found evidence to suggest that video game play cultivates sexist beliefs, the sexist and misogynistic culture of many online gaming communities has been well documented. The websites *Not in the Kitchen Anymore*[73] and *Fat, Ugly, or Slutty*[74] have chronicled some of these incidents over the last few years. A quick browse of these sites' homepages gives a snapshot of the offensive and abusive comments that have been directed toward female video game players, including verbal sexual assaults, gender-based insults, and requests for sexual favors.

ALMOST 80 PERCENT OF ALL GAME PLAYERS BELIEVE THAT SEXISM IS PROMINENT WITHIN THE GAMING COMMUNITY.

The comments archived on the websites *Not in the Kitchen Anymore* and *Fat, Ugly or Slutty* are too graphic to share in this book.

IT IS UNCLEAR WHY THESE KINDS OF CULTURES HAVE DEVELOPED.

While one might quickly dismiss this archived evidence as being representative of only the more extreme cases, almost 80 percent of all game players believe that sexism is prominent within the gaming community[75].

63 percent of female players report that they have experienced sexist or misogynistic behavior from other players[76].

It is unclear why these kinds of cultures have developed. One theory is that male players feel threatened by female players, especially those who are more skilled[77]. Another theory is that as video games have long been a "boy's toy"[78], so the growing popularity of video games among females is threatening what has long been considered a man's domain[79].

Take Home Message

Video games may have the power to reinforce sexist beliefs and attitudes in the short term, but there is no research to suggest that they will be cultivated or magnified over time among players who did not hold these beliefs to a certain extent to begin with. However, while video games may not cultivate these beliefs through their male-centered content, the sexist and misogynistic undertones of many online gaming cultures have been well documented by researchers and players. Today, more than half of all female players report having experienced some form of sex-based harassment while playing online games.

THE SEXIST AND MISOGYNISTIC CULTURE OF MANY ONLINE GAMING COMMUNITIES HAS BEEN WELL DOCUMENTED.

Advice To Parents

It is important to speak with your children about discrimination toward women and to let them know that they may be exposed to sexist and misogynistic attitudes and behaviors while playing online. It is also **ENCOURAGE YOUR CHILDREN TO REPORT ALL DISCRIMINATORY BEHAVIOR AND HARASSMENT.**

important to tell your children that if they witness this kind of harassment directly or indirectly, they should not sit idly by. Encourage your children to report all discriminatory behavior and/or harassment to the game moderators (various reporting features are built in to specific games and gaming platforms). Far too often these kinds of behaviors are ignored, possibility because of desensitization to these kinds of comments or a general complacency with the presence of this behavior within gamer cultures, or both. By taking a stand, we are taking the first steps towards seeing this kind of behavior diminish and, hopefully, fall out of favor.

6

Social Outcomes

O nline friends are often thought of as being weaker than their offline counterparts, in terms of their ability to provide social and emotional support. This leads to fears that socializing and making friends online, particularly through online gaming, might detrimentally impact players' offline friendships in the short term and could even deteriorate their offline social skills in the long term. While this scenario paints online gaming as a dangerous, slippery slope, scientific research in this area suggests that these fears are likely misplaced.

❓ What impact will online game play have on my child's offline friendships?

Childhood and adolescence is an important period of social development. Important social abilities, such as learning to create and maintain close friendships and to read body language, are developed during this time (for example, the knowledge that maintaining eye

FRIENDSHIPS PLAY AN INTEGRAL ROLE IN SOCIAL DEVELOPMENT.

contact and leaning in while chatting likely indicates interest in the conversation)[80,81]. Friendships play an integral role in social development, as they provide many opportunities for social observation, rehearsal, and feedback. Through observation, children and adolescents learn what is socially appropriate and inappropriate[82,83]. Rehearsal and feedback then provide them with the opportunity to develop, hone, and master their own social abilities.

THROUGH OBSERVATION, CHILDREN AND ADOLESCENTS LEARN WHAT IS SOCIALLY APPROPRIATE AND INAPPROPRIATE.

The problem that comes with making friends online is that, because there are only so many hours in the day, players who spend more time online are spending less time offline. Over time, this could lead to an exchange or displacement of

offline for online friendships. In turn, that can have a range of negative social effects, such as the loss of friendships and a potential deterioration of or failure to develop effective social skills for the real world.

Evidence of displacement effects has been found, as adolescents who play video games report spending less time with their parents and friends than those who do not play video games[84]. Increased social online video game play has also been associated with smaller offline social circles for adolescent players[85]. Experimental studies have found that,

MANY CHILDREN REPORT PLAYING ONLINE GAMES WITH THEIR PARENTS, FAMILY MEMBERS, AND OFFLINE FRIENDS.

after one month of playing online games, players began to place greater value on their online friends than their offline ones[86]. Declines were also evidenced in how often friends came to visit and the frequency at which gamers themselves visited friends and relatives[87].

It should be noted, however, that none of the research studies discussed above measured the actual exchange of offline friends for online ones over time. Furthermore, they did not account for the fact that many children and adolescents report playing online games with their parents, family members, and preexisting, offline friends[1,88]. In these cases, playing online games would likely serve as a fun activity to do together and, over time, could serve to strengthen these social relationships.

40% of players report playing with (pre-existing/offline) friends, **21%** with family members, **17%** with parents[1].

Taking the research as a whole, it is likely that online game play only temporarily impacts the time spent with offline friends. A lack of long-term impact is further supported by the fact that global differences have not been found in the overall size or quality of friendship circles between online, offline, and non–video game playing groups[49,88].

Will playing online games cause my child to lose offline social skills?

Parents are becoming increasingly concerned about the long-term effects of online video game play on the social skills of their children. As face-to-face communication is key to developing a range of social abilities[89], it is a reasonable concern. Spending endless hours socializing online could hinder the development of offline or real-world social skills, such as being able to start a conversation with a stranger or being aware of and using appropriate body language. The latter is of particular concern as non-verbal cues are typically absent when socializing online unless they are explicitly communicated through in-game gesturing systems or text-based emoticons. While the use of such tools can accommodate for a substantial proportion of non-verbal cues that are often missing in online

NON-VERBAL CUES ARE TYPICALLY ABSENT WHEN SOCIALIZING ONLINE.

communication (such as body positioning and eye contact), it still creates a world in which verbal and non-verbal cues are disjoined[90]. This is in stark contrast to face-to-face communication, where our clothing, posture, facial expressions, and other non-verbal cues provide others with a range of information, such as our personality traits, level of agreeableness, and self-esteem[91].

Researchers have found that those players who report a higher amount of weekly play time are less socially expressive than their counterparts. For

FACE-TO-FACE COMMUNICATION IS KEY TO DEVELOPING A RANGE OF SOCIAL ABILITIES.

example, they may have a lower ability to verbally express themselves; starting and maintaining verbal conversation may be difficult[92]. They may also be more emotionally sensitive to nonverbal cues, which is a sign of shyness[93].

eg Someone who is emotionally sensitive may be more likely to interpret a friend's sudden move to a crossed-arm position as disinterest or defensiveness rather than simply a shift in body position.

However, when researchers have followed the same players over time, no direct connection between online video game use and social skills has been found[94], even among problematic and addicted players[95].

NO DIRECT CONNECTION BETWEEN ONLINE VIDEO GAME USE AND SOCIAL SKILLS HAS BEEN FOUND.

Taken together, this research suggests that, rather than video games leading to a deterioration of social skills, individuals who are less socially expressive and more emotionally sensitive may be more likely to play online video games because of the range of social accommodation gaming provides.

eg The visual anonymity provided by online games (the idea that "you can't see me") removes many social obstacles relating to social self-presentation (the ability to interpret and convey appropriate body language) that may have hindered successful face-to-face communication, especially for those who are shy or otherwise less socially skilled[93,96-99].

❓ Do online video games promote feelings of loneliness?

Concerns of video games contributing to feelings of loneliness have been fueled by the stereotype of the lonely, reclusive, and socially inept basement-dwelling video game player[56]. These days, this unflattering prototype is more often attributed to the online gamer[100] than the offline gamer because of newfound fears that electronic friendships provide a superficial sense of support and displace time that could be spent fostering more meaningful, offline relationships[92,101].

VIDEO GAME PLAY HAS NOT BEEN FOUND TO BE A DIRECT CONTRIBUTOR TO INCREASED LONELINESS.

LONELINESS HAS BEEN FOUND TO MOTIVATE AND EVEN WORSEN THEIR PROBLEMATIC ONLINE GAME PLAY OVER TIME.

Lending support to these claims, research has found that lonely individuals are more likely to play online games than individuals who are not lonely[92].

However, when following those same players over time, video game play has not been found to be a direct contributor to increased loneliness[94]. This makes sense, since these fears are often based on the assumption that players are exchanging their offline friends for online ones, and that, as noted above, is not supported by scientific research in this area. There is one exception, however, and that is adolescent, problematic/addicted players. For these players, loneliness has been found to motivate and even worsen their problematic online game play over time[95].

Take Home Message

Claims that online game play can have global, devastating, and long-term social consequences have been taken out of context and exaggerated. Researchers have noted that more frequent online game play is associated with less time spent with friends and family; however, this is likely because there are only so many hours in a day, and if you are spending time

CLAIMS THAT ONLINE GAME PLAY CAN HAVE LONG-TERM SOCIAL CONSEQUENCES HAVE BEEN EXAGGERATED.

 doing one thing, you are inevitably spending less time doing another. Long-term consequences— loss of close friendships, deterioration of social skills, and increased loneliness—have not been found to be a direct after effect of online game play, with the exception of loneliness worsening over time among problematic, adolescent players.

Advice To Parents

While online video game play has not been directly linked to long-term negative social outcomes, socializing and playing exclusively with online friends for extended periods of time could strain some friendships, especially with those who do not play games. Balance is key here. So while you need not be overly worried that online gaming will ruin your children's social lives, you should still keep them engaged in face-to-face activities with their friends as well, even if that activity involves more video games.

KEEP THEM ENGAGED IN FACE-TO-FACE ACTIVITIES WITH FRIENDS, EVEN IF THAT ACTIVITY INVOLVES VIDEO GAMES.

7

Unintentional
(Positive) Learning

While the focus of media-effects research has long been on what negative thoughts, attitudes, and behaviors video games might teach players, researchers have recently turned their attention to the potential positive learning experiences that can occur when playing video games. This is referred to as unintentional learning because the players are not playing the game with the explicit goal of learning something new. Research has found that video games are great vehicles for learning new fields of knowledge, skills, and abilities.

❓ How does video game play promote learning?

Part of the reason video games are such great vehicles for learning is because they induce a state of flow. Colloquially referred to as being "in the zone," players experience flow states when the in-game challenges are balanced with the skill level of the player[102].

ANXIETY

FLOW

BOREDOM

LEVEL OF CHALLENGE

LEVEL OF SKILL

IT MUST BE RECOGNIZED THAT GAMES ARE GREAT VEHICLES FOR LEARNING.

When in a state of flow, players become hyperfocused, experience a distortion of time and space, and are driven to continue playing because they are having a good time. If you have played video games before, you have likely experienced this flow state. For example, have you ever gotten up from a gaming session only to be surprised at how much time had flown by? Perhaps you thought you had played for an hour, but really three hours had passed. You were likely in a flow state!

When in a flow state, various kinds of learning can occur. This is because the player is hyperfocused on the in-game tasks and is determined to complete them because his or her skill levels are being challenged.

Of course, it must also be recognized that games are great vehicles for learning because people want to play them. Video games are popular activities for children and adolescents because they are fun to play. Furthermore, playing with friends can socially reinforce the activity, making them want to play more. In this sense, video games create ideal learning groups, as children and adolescents want to engage with them.

VIDEO GAMES ARE GREAT AT BALANCING IN-GAME CHALLENGES AND THE SKILL LEVEL.

What skills or abilities have video games been found to unintentionally teach?

Researchers have found that video game play can help promote a variety of skills and abilities such as creative thinking, problem solving, time management, and leadership skills[103].

The links between video game play and creative thinking may not be particularly surprising, as most video games require players to develop new solutions to different problems in a short amount of time. Whether you are exploring a new world, solving a puzzle, or figuring out how to best

OVERCOMING IN-GAME CHALLENGES CAN PROMOTE CREATIVE THINKING.

craft a new object, overcoming the various in-game challenges can promote creative thinking and can help develop more complex problem solving skills[103].

 Researchers have called for a greater recognition of video games as powerful tools for encouraging positive outcomes[103].

LEADERSHIP SKILLS CAN ALSO BE DEVELOPED AND HONED THROUGH VIDEO GAME PLAY.

Leadership skills can also be developed and honed through video game play, especially when playing online in mixed-

age teams. Online gaming provides a particularly unique opportunity to observe, learn, and practice leading groups of all sizes, ages, and backgrounds[39]. For some children and adolescents, it may be their only opportunity to lead a group of adults to victory. Experimenting with and experiencing success in leadership roles while online has also been found to cross over into other offline contexts[104,105]. In fact, many large corporations have begun considering online leadership experience equivalent to offline counterparts and have begun to actively advertise for applicants with experience leading virtual groups[106].

 "If you want to see what business leadership may look like in three to five years, look at what's happening in online games"

Byron Reeves

Professor of Communication at Stanford University

Children and adolescents can also unintentionally pick up a range of new knowledge while playing video games, the nature of which depends on the particular game they are playing. For instance, players can learn about history by playing games such as those in the *Age of Empires* series (Microsoft Studios), or they can learn what it

CHILDREN AND ADOLESCENTS CAN UNINTENTIONALLY PICK UP A RANGE OF NEW KNOWLEDGE WHILE PLAYING VIDEO GAMES.

takes to be a successful city planner by playing the popular simulation series, *Sim City* (Electronic Arts). Players of my generation often remember the game *Civilization* (Sid Meyer) as a valuable tool for learning world history, key world leaders, and the ancient wonders of the world.

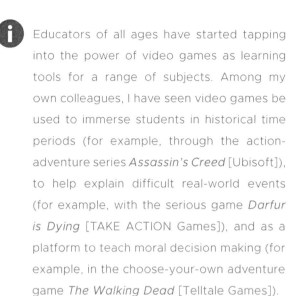 Educators of all ages have started tapping into the power of video games as learning tools for a range of subjects. Among my own colleagues, I have seen video games be used to immerse students in historical time periods (for example, through the action-adventure series *Assassin's Creed* [Ubisoft]), to help explain difficult real-world events (for example, with the serious game *Darfur is Dying* [TAKE ACTION Games]), and as a platform to teach moral decision making (for example, in the choose-your-own adventure game *The Walking Dead* [Telltale Games]).

Take Home Message

When it comes to research on video game effects, the results are not all doom and gloom. Video games have been found to be great vehicles for learning new information, skills, and abilities. While visual-spatial skills are often the focus when discussing the positive learning effects of gaming (see Chapter 3), creative thinking, problem solving, and leadership skills have also been found to be refined through video game play.

VIDEO GAMES HAVE BEEN FOUND TO BE GREAT VEHICLES FOR LEARNING NEW INFORMATION, SKILLS, AND ABILITIES.

Advice to Parents

Talk to your children about what draws them to their favorite games to see what things they might be learning. Are they leading groups to success online? Becoming strategic war generals? Learning how to be creative with scraps in the postapocalyptic world? Talking to your children about their favorite video games can be a great jumping-off point for a range of new activities to do together. For instance, they might be interested in taking their puzzle-solving prowess

TALK TO YOUR CHILDREN ABOUT THEIR FAVORITE VIDEO GAMES.

to a local escape-room experience, or maybe they'd like to test out their battlefield skills at a paintballing event. For teenagers, this can be especially valuable, as it can sometimes be difficult to find fun (read: cool) things to do as a family.

Additional
Reading

If you would like to delve a bit deeper into the science of game studies and media-effects research, here are several recommendations for further reading.

If you are interested in video game effects research in general, I suggest picking up a copy of *The Video Game Debate: Unravelling the Physical, Social, and Psychological Effects of Digital Games*, a book I coedited with Thorsten Quandt. This book provides a series of essays relating to all of the topics discussed here (and more), written by experts from each particular field of research. Created with a general audience in mind, this book is a good read for nonscientific audiences.

Getting Gamers: The Psychology of Video Games and Their Impact on the People Who Play Them, by Jamie Madigan, is another good choice if you are looking for a general overview of game-studies research. While this book does not focus specifically on media effects, it does discuss a range of topics associated with video game play, including why people act differently online and the allure of violent video games. The book is insightful, entertaining, and a perfect choice for the casual reader.

If you are interested in learning more about a specific topic discussed in this book, here are a few of my top picks.

For more about video games and aggression/violence, I recommend *Grand Theft Childhood*, by Lawrence Kutner and Cheryl K. Olson. This book provides an in-depth discussion of the research in this area, breaking down the science behind the often sensationalized headlines.

I also recommend the new book *Moral Combat: Why the War on Violent Video Games is Wrong* by Patrick M. Markey and Christopher J. Ferguson. Drawing from the most recent research in the area, this book outlines how the media has been wrong to cultivate a culture of fear about this new, interactive media through blaming video games for real-world crime. This book also includes practical advice for parents, including tips on how to reduce the amount of time your children spend playing video games.

For more about games and cognitive development, consider picking up a copy of *What Video Games Have to Teach Us about Learning and Literacy*, by James Paul Gee. This book does a great job of presenting underlying theories and real-world examples of how even violent video games can contribute to cognitive learning and development.

For more about video game addiction, I would suggest skipping the many self-diagnosis books on the market. Instead, choose *Hooked on Games: The Lure and Cost of Video Game and Internet Addiction*, by Andrew P. Doan and Brooke Strickland. This book gives a unique look into video game addiction by taking a biographical approach and drawing on Dr. Doan's own struggles with addiction.

For more about video games and social outcomes, I recommend *Multiplayer: The Social Aspects of Digital Gaming*, edited by Thorsten Quandt and Sonja Kröger. This book presents a series of essays that range in focus from an overview of the various social interactions in virtual worlds, to research on online gaming and colocated play, to the unique pitfalls of social play. This book is a great resource if you are looking for a well-rounded understanding of the various uses and potential impacts of social gaming both off- and online.

I also suggest picking up a copy of *Leet Noobs*, by Mark Chen. This book does not focus on media effects, but rather on social connections and the sense of camaraderie that can form between players of online games. The book follows a group of *World of Warcraft* players over a period of ten months. Dr. Chen documents the interactions and relationships between these online game players and highlights the overlooked side of online gaming, including the close interpersonal relationships and strong group camaraderie that can form. It is a compelling book that demonstrates the evolution of gaming communities and the social connections that can form within them.

If you are looking for something a bit more informal, there are several blogs, podcasts, and *YouTube* channels focused on game studies that regularly publish features about video game effects. Here are some of my top picks.

The Psychology of Games Blog and Podcast
www.PsychologyofGames.com
Created by Dr. Jamie Madigan, *The Psychology of Games* regularly posts articles and podcasts about a range of topics that fall under the game studies umbrella. These podcasts are always entertaining and feature some of the top scholars in game studies across a wide variety of academic disciplines.

PBS Game/Show YouTube Channel
www.youtube.com/user/pbsgameshow
While this channel is no longer active, their short, entertaining

videos about all things games remain archived on YouTube. Their videos tackle a wide range of topics relating to video games and modern life, including interviews with industry professionals, discussions of the representation of women in games, and current debates about video games. While new content is no longer being created, this channel still has a little bit of something for everyone.

Chris Ferguson's Huffington Post Blog
www.huffingtonpost.com/author/cjfergus-24

Dr. Christopher Ferguson (Stetson University) contributes articles for the *Huffington Post* relating to video game research. His articles encompass a range of topics, from violent video games and desensitization to breaking down policy statements about video game regulation.

Feminist Frequency YouTube Channel
www.youtube.com/user/feministfrequency

Created by Anita Sarkeesian, this *YouTube* channel produces high-quality videos that explore the representation of women in video games. It also provides occasional video game reviews. While it is a bit more of a niche site, the videos on this channel are insightful, well made, and full of information. I learn something new every time I watch one.

The personal blog of Mark Griffiths
www.drmarkgriffiths.wordpress.com

Professor Mark Griffiths (Nottingham Trent University) is a behavioral addiction specialist and one of the world's preeminent researchers on video game addiction. His blog features informative, easy to read, and always interesting articles relating to addictive, obsessional, compulsive, and extreme behaviors.

Concluding Thoughts

I hope that this guide was able to provide some insight into the science behind the video game headlines. The aim was to quell fears and put to rest some long-standing debates relating to video game effects. While the research findings present a lot less doom and gloom than some media outlets may have you believe, you should still be mindful of the media forms your children are consuming. Just as you would take note of which movies they are watching, you should be aware of which video games they are playing as well.

A common concern raised by parents is whether the games their children are playing are age appropriate. In the United States, the Entertainment Software Ratings Board (ESRB) is responsible for assigning age-rating categories, content descriptors, and pointing out the interactive content for any given video game title. These designations are clearly marked on video game packaging and are there to help parents select appropriate games for their children by identifying the content included in any particular video game title. Visit their website (*www.esrb.org*) for more information on age ratings, content descriptors, and interactive content. If you are located in the European Union, visit the PEGI (Pan European Game Information) website (*www.pegi.info*), as they are responsible for European game rating standards.

The best way to know what kind of games your children are playing is to play with them. Not a fan of video games? That's okay! You can just be in the room when they play. You may be surprised how your children open up (about a range of things) when you show interest in what interests them.

Frequently Asked Questions

What makes a game a "video game"?

A video game is a digital game played by electronically manipulating images produced by software on a display screen. This includes games created with original content as well as digital forms of traditional card and board games. Video games are commonly played on personal computers, gaming consoles (e.g., *PlayStation, Xbox, Nintendo Wii U*), handheld gaming platforms (e.g., *Nintendo DS, Sony PSP*), and electronic devices that are not dedicated game-playing machines, such as smart phones.

Video games are available in a variety of genre categories ranging from casual games (ones that does not require a large time commitment or a special set of skills to complete), to more complex role-playing games (ones where a player assumes the role of a character in a fictional setting and acts out the character's role).

> If you are interested in learning more about video game genres, Wikipedia has generated a comprehensive list of genre categories and their descriptions. You can find that list here, *https://en.wikipedia.org/wiki/List_of_video_game_genres*

An online video game is a video game that is either partially or primarily played through the Internet or another connected network. Unlike traditional video games, online games are typically designed to encourage and facilitate social interactions among players through cooperation, competition, or both.

Are all online gamers lonely, basement dwellers?

As I hope you have already gleamed from this chapter, online gaming is not synonymous with all of the doom and gloom associated with it. This is especially true when it comes to the stereotype of online gamers.

Stereotypes are sets of associations between categories and traits (for example, online gamers [category] are pale [trait]). Once learned, they become relatively fixed and are automatically drawn upon when processing information about people from any particular social category.

Perhaps in part because of its rapid growth in popularity, online gaming is an activity that has come to be associated with a highly specific, caricatured, and negative image[56,92,100]. Often portrayed as unpopular, unattractive, lazy, and socially inept, the stereotype of the online gamers are truly the least desirable subgroup of "gamers".

 A 2012 study investigating the stereotypes of various gaming groups found that console gamers are perceived significantly less stereotypically than online gamers and online gaming subgroups, such as MMORPG players[100].

But how accurate is the portrayal of online gamers? Turns out, not very accurate[49]. In a 2014 research study, online game players were not found to have fewer friends, less social support, less social ability, or less frequent exercise than offline or non-game players[49].

Do you have any specific "family friendly" game recommendations?

As everybody has different preferences when it comes to video games, it is difficult to make specific recommendations. However, if you are looking for video games to play together as a family, I would suggest games that fall in the "party" genre. These kinds of games are typically designed for four or more players, making them perfect for a family game night. Popular series' in the party genre include Rock Band (Electronic Arts) and Hasbro Family Game Night (Electronic Arts).

How can I be sure I am choosing age appropriate games for my child?

One of the most common concerns raised by parents is making sure that the games their children are playing are age-appropriate. In the United States, the Entertainment Software Ratings Board (*ESRB*) is responsible for assigning age-rating categories and content descriptors to video games. These designations are clearly marked on video game packaging and are there to help parents select an appropriate game for their children by identifying the content that is included in any particular video game title.

Age Ratings and Content Descriptors

Currently the *ESRB* uses six age category distinctions to identify the age-appropriateness of any particular video game:

EC - Early Childhood
Content is intended for young children.

E - Everyone
Content is generally suitable for all ages. May contain minimal cartoon, fantasy or mild violence and/or infrequent use of mild language.

E 10+ - Everyone 10+
Content is generally suitable for ages 10 and up. May contain more cartoon, fantasy or mild violence, mild language and/or minimal suggestive themes.

T - Teen
Content is generally suitable for ages 13 and up. May contain violence, suggestive themes, crude humor, minimal blood, simulated gambling and/or infrequent use of strong language.

M - Mature
Content is generally suitable for ages 17 and up. May contain intense violence, blood and gore, sexual content and/or strong language.

AO - Adults Only 18+

Content suitable only for adults ages 18 and up. May include prolonged scenes of intense violence, graphic sexual content and/or gambling with real currency. Content Descriptors and Interactive Elements.

When deciding which game may be right for your child, it is important to not only note the age rating but also the game content. To help with this, the *ESRB* has lists content descriptors next to the age rating on the video game packaging. There are currently more than two-dozen content descriptors used by the *ESRB* ranging from general descriptors, such as "mature humor" to specific inclusions, such as "Use of Tobacco".

With the popularization of online gaming, the *ESRB* has begun adding labels for interactive elements. These are typically listed in a separate box from the age rating and content descriptors. These labels identify the online content of the game and provide information about whether or not a particular allows players to interact with other players online and if the game will share information about the player, including their location, to the rest of the gaming network.

 Location sharing is this feature is typically enabled by default (and can often only be restricted by changing the privacy settings on the game console itself).

For more information on age ratings, content descriptors, and interactive content, you can visit the *ESRB* website at *www.ESRB.org.*

References

1. Entertainment Software Association. Essential Facts About the Computer and Video Game Industry. 2016:1-16.

2. TMachine.org. More than 1 billion people play online games in 2008. *T=Machine Internet Gaming, Comput Games, Technol MMO, Web 20*. 2008. Available at: *http://t-machine.org/index.php/2008/11/18/more-than-1-billion-people-play-online-games-in-2008/*.

3. Nizza M. Tying Columbine to Video Games. *nytimes.com*. 2007. Available at: *http://thelede.blogs.nytimes.com/2007/07/05/tieing-columbine-to-video-games/*.

4. Adams M. Batman movie massacre a reflection of violent video games, TSA violence against citizens and psychiatric drugging of young white men. *naturalnews.com*. 2012. Available at: *http://www.naturalnews.com/036535_Batman_massacre_shooting.html*.

5. Greene L, Golding B. Lanza prepared with "school shooting" game. *New York Post*. *http://nypost.com/2013/11/25/sandy-hook-shooter-obsessed-with-columbine/*. Published November 25, 2013.

6. Strasburger VC, Wilson BJ, Jordan AB. *Children, Adolescents, and the Media*. 3rd ed. London: Sage; 2014.

7. Villani S. Impact of Media on Children and Adolescents: A 10-Year Review of the Research. *J Am Acad Child Adolesc Psychiatry*. 2001;40(4):392-401. doi:10.1097/00004583-200104000-00007.

8. Earles KA, Alexander R, Johnson M, Liverpool J, McGhee M. Media influences on children and adolescents: violence and sex. *J Natl Med Assoc*. 2002;94(9):797-801.

9. American Psychiatric Association. *Diagnostic and Statistical Manual of Mental Disorders*. Washington D.C.: American Psychiatric Association; 2000.

10. King DL, Delfabbro PH, D GM. Video game addiction. In: Miller P, ed. *Principles of Addiction: Comprehensive Addictive Behaviors and Disorders*. San Diego: Academic Press; 2013:819-825.

11. Griffiths MD. Gaming Addiction & Internet Gaming Disorder. In: Kowert R, Quandt T, eds. *The Video Game Debate: Unravelling the Physical, Social, and Psychological Effects of Digital Games*. New York: Routledge; 2016:74-93.

12. Gentile DA. Pathological video-game use among youth ages 8 to 18: a national study. *Psychol Sci.* 2009;20:594-602.

13. Festl R, Scharkow M, Quandt T. Problematic computer game use among adolescents, younger and older adults. *Addiction.* 2012:592-599. doi:10.1111/add.12016.

14. Griffiths MD. A "components" model of addiction within a biopsychosocial framework. *J Subst Use.* 2005;10(4):191-197.

15. Kardefeld-Winther, D. Commentary on: Are we overpathologizing everyday life? A tenable blueprint for behavioral addiction research. *J Behav Addict.* 2015;4:126-129. doi:10.1556/2006.4.2015.019.

16. Van Rooij AJ, Van Looy J, Billieux J. Internet Gaming Disorder as a formative construct: Implications for conceptualization and measurement. *Psychiatry Clin Neurosci.* 2016:1-14. doi:doi. org/10.1111/pcn.12404.

17. Charlton JP. A factor-analytic investigation of computer "addiction" and engagement. *Br J Psychol.* 2002;93:329-344.

18. Ferguson CJ, Ceranoglu TA. Attention Problems and Pathological Gaming: Resolving the "Chicken and Egg" in a Prospective Analysis. *Psychiatr Q.* 2014;85(1):103-110.

19. King DL, Delfabbro PH, Griffiths MD. Clinical interventions for technology-based problems: Excessive Internet and video game use. *J Cogn Psychother.* 2012;26:43-56.

20. Ferguson CJ, Kilburn J. Much ado about nothing: the misestimation and overinterpretation of violent video game effects in eastern and western nations: comment on Anderson et al. (2010). *Psychol Bull.* 2010;136:174-178-187. doi:10.1037/a0018566.

21. Roskos-Ewoldsen DR, Roskos-Ewoldsen, B. Carpentier FD. Media priming: A synthesis. In: Bryant J, Zillmann D, eds. *Media Effects: Advances in Theory and Research,.* 3rd ed. New York: Taylor and Francis; 2009:74-93.

22. Barlett CP, Anderson CA, Swing EL. Video Game Effects—Confirmed, Suspected, and Speculative. *Simul Gaming.* 2009;40(3):377-403.

23. Coulson M, Ferguson CJ. The Influence of Digital Games on Aggression and Violent Crime. In: Kowert R, Quandt T, eds.

The Video Game Debate: Unravelling the Physical, Social, and Psychological Effects of Digital Games. New York: Routledge; 2016:54-73.

24. Elson M, Ferguson CJ. Twenty-Five Years of Research on Violence in Digital Games and Aggression. *Eur Psychol.* 2013;19(1):1-14.

25. Hull JG, Brunelle TJ, Prescott AT, Sargent JD. A longitudinal study of risk-glorifying video games and behavioral deviance. *2014.* 107:300-325. doi:10.1037/a0036058.

26. Von Salisch M, Vogelgesang J, Kristen A, Oppl C. Preference for violent electronic games and aggressive behavior among children: The beginning of the downward spiral? *Media Psychol.* 2011;14:233-258. doi:10.1080/15213269.2011.596468.

27. Wallenius M, Punamaki R-L. Digital game violence and direct aggression in adolescence: A longitudinal study of the roles of sex, age, and parent-child communication. *J Appl Dev Psychol.* 2008;29:261-294. doi:10.1016/j.appdev.2008.04.010.

28. Ferguson CJ, Garza A, Jerabeck J, Ramos R, Galindo M. Not worth the fuss after all? cross-sectional and prospective data on violent video game influences on aggression, visuospatial cognition and mathematics ability in a sample of youth. *J Youth Adolesc.* 2013;42(1):109-122. doi:10.1007/s10964-012-9803-6.

29. Ferguson CJ, Colwell J. A Meaner, More Callous Digital World for Youth? The Relationship Between Violent Digital Games, Motivation, Bullying, and Civic Behavior Among Children. *Psychol Pop Media Cult.* 2016. doi:10.1037/ppm0000128.

30. Breuer J, Vogelgesang J, Quandt T, Festl R. Violent video games and physical aggression: Evidence for a selection effect among adolescents. *Psychol Pop Media Cult.* 2015;4:305-328. doi:10.1037/ppm0000035.

31. Ritter D, Eslea M. Hot sauce, toy guns, and graffiti: A critical account of current laboratory aggression paradigms. *Aggress Behav.* 2005;31:407-419.

32. Anderson CA, Carnagey NL, Flanagan M, Benjamin AJ, Eubanks J, Valentine JC. Violent videogames: Specific effects of violent content on aggressive thoughts and behavior. In: Zanna M, ed. *Advances in Experimental Social Psychology.* New York: Elsevier; 2004:199-249.

33. Sestir MA, Bartholow BD. Violent and nonviolent video games produce opposing effects on aggressive and prosocial outcomes. *J Exp Soc Psychol.* 2010;46:934-942. doi:0.1016/j.jesp.2010.06.005.

34. Lieberman JD, Solomon S, Greenberg J, McGregor HA. A hot new way to measure aggression: Hot sauce allocation. *Aggress Behav.* 1999;25:331-348.

35. Bennerstedt U, Ivarsson J, Linderoth J. How gamers manage aggression: Situating skills in collaborative computer games. *Comput Collab Learn.* 2011;7(1):43-61.

36. Bowen HJ, Spaniol J. Chronic exposure to violent video games is not associated with alterations of emotional memory. *Appl Cogn Psychol.* 2011;25(6):906-916. doi:10.1002/acp.1767.

37. Grizzard M, Tamborini R, Sherry JL, Weber R. Repeated Play Reduces Video Games' Ability to Elicit Guilt: Evidence from a Longitudinal Experiment. *Media Psychol.* 2016:1-24.

38. Tear MJ, Nielsen M. Failure to Demonstrate That Playing Violent Video Games Diminishes Prosocial Behavior. *PLoS One.* 2013. doi:10.1371/journal.pone.0068382.

39. Olson CK. Are Electronic Games Health Hazards or Health Promoters? In: Kowert R, Quandt T, eds. *The Video Game Debate: Unravelling the Physical, Social, and Psychological Effects of Digital Games.* New York: Routledge; 2016:39-53.

40. Oakley L. *Cognitive Development.* New York: Routledge; 2004.

41. Dale G, Green CS. Video Games and Cognitive Performance. In: Kowert R, Quandt T, eds. *The Video Game Debate: Unravelling the Physical, Social, and Psychological Effects of Digital Games.* New York: Routledge; 2016:131-152.

42. Adachi P, Willoughby T. Do video games promote positive youth development? *J Adolesc Res.* 2012;28:155-165.

43. Bergen D. The role of pretend play in children's cognitive development. *Early Child Res Pract.* 2002;4(1).

44. Moore M, Russ SW. Follow-up of a pretend play intervention: Effects on play, creativity, and emotional processes in children. *Creat Res J.* 2008;20(4):427-436.

45. Spence I, Feng J. Video games and spatial cognition. *Rev Gen Psychol.* 2010;14:92-104.

46. Ferguson CJ. Blazing Angels or Resident Evil? Can Violent Video Games Be a Force for Good? *Rev Gen Psychol.* 2010;14(2):68-81.

47. Physical Activity Council. *2016 Participation Report.*; 2016. Available at: *http://www.physicalactivitycouncil.com/pdfs/current.pdf.*

48. Williams D, Yee N, Caplan S. Who plays, how much, and why? Debunking the stereotypical gamer profile. *J Comput Commun Monogr.* 2008;13(4):993-1018. doi:10.1111/j.1083-6101.2008.00428.x.

49. Kowert R, Festl R, Quandt T. Unpopular, Overweight, and Socially Inept: Reconsidering the Stereotype of Online Gamers. *Cyberpsychology, Behav Soc Netw.* 2013;17(3):141-146. doi:10.1089/cyber.2013.0118.

50. Gao Z, Chen S. Are field-based exergames useful in preventing childhood obesity? *Obes Rev.* 2014;15(8):676-691.

51. LeBlanc AG, Chaput J-P, McFarlane A, et al. Active Video Games and Health Indicators in Children and Youth: A Systematic Review. *PLoS One.* 2013;8(6).

52. Labrique A, Carabas Y, Carras MC. Pokémon GO!—Pandemic or Prescription? The Public Health Perspective. *Glob Heal Now.* 2016. Available at: *http://www.globalhealthnow.org/news/pokmon-go-pandemic-or-prescription-the-public-health-perspective.*

53. Tsukayama H. Pokemon Go's unexpected side effect: Injuries*The Washington Post. https://www.washingtonpost.com/news/the-switch/wp/2016/07/08/pokemon-gos-unexpected-side-effect-injuries/.* Published July 10, 2016.

54. Cardoso-Leite P, Bavelier D. Video game play, attention, and learning: how to shape the development of attention and influence learning? *Curr Opin Neurol.* 2014;27(2). doi:10.1097/WCO.0000000000000077.

55. Prins PJ, Dovis S, Ponsioen A, ten Brink E, van der Oord S. Does computerized working memory training with game elements enhance motivation and training efficacy in children with ADD? *Cyberpsychology, Behav Soc Netw.* 2011;14(3). doi:10.1089/cyber.2009.0206.

56.   Kowert R, Griffiths MD, Oldmeadow JA. Geek or Chic? Emerging Stereotypes of Online Gamers. *Bull Sci Technol Soc.* 2012;32(6):471-479. doi:10.1177/0270467612469078.

57.   Caplan S, Williams D, Yee N. Problematic Internet use and psychosocial well-being among MMO players. *Comput Human Behav.* 2009;25(6):1312-1319. doi:10.1016/j.chb.2009.06.006.

58.   Lo S, Wang C, Fang W. Physical Interpersonal Relationships and Social Anxiety among Online Game Players. *Cyberpsychology Behav.* 2005;8(1):15-20. doi:10.1089/cpb.2005.8.15.

59.   Kim E, Namkoong K, Ku T, Kim S. The relationship between online game addiction and aggression, self-control, and narcissistic personality traits. *Eur Psychiatry.* 2008;23(3):212-218. doi:10.1016/j.eurpsy.2007.10.010.

60.   Gentile DA, Choo H, Liau A, et al. Pathological video game use among youths: a two-year longitudinal study. *Pediatrics.* 2011.

61.   Mentzoni RA, Brunborg GS, Molde H, et al. Problematic video game use: estimated prevalence and associations with mental and physical health. Cyberpsychology, *Behav Soc Netw.* 2011;14(10):591-596.

62.   Glaubke CR, Miller P, Parker MA, Espejo E. Fair Play? Violence, Gender, and *Race in Video Games.* Children NOW; 2001. Available at: *http://files.eric.ed.gov/fulltext/ED463092.pdf.*

63.   Waddell TF, Ivory JD, Conde R, Long C, McDonnell R. White Man's Virtual World: A Systematic Content Analysis of Gender and Race in Massively Multiplayer Online Games. *J Virtual Worlds Res.* 2014;7(2):1-14. doi:10.4101/jvwr.v7i2.7096.

64.   Beasley B, Standley TC. Shirts vs. Skins: Clothing as an Indicator of Gender Role Stereotyping in Video Games. *Mass Commun Soc.* 2002;5(3):279-293.

65.   Dill K, Thill KP. Video Game Characters and the Socialization of Gender Roles: Young People's Perceptions Mirror Sexist Media Depictions. *Sex Roles.* 2007;57:851-864.

66.   Dickey MD. Girl gamers: the controversy of girl games and the relevance of female oriented design for instructional design. *Br J Educ Technol.* 2006;37(5):785-793.

67. Sarkeesian A. Tropes vs. Women in Video Games. 2013. Available at: *https://www.youtube.com/watch?v=X6p5AZp7r_Q*.

68. Gerbner G, Gross L, Morgan M, Singnorielli N. Growing up with television: The cultivation perspective BT - Media effects: Advances in theory and research. In: Bryant J, Zillman D, eds. *Media Effects: Advances in Theory and Research*. Hillsdale: Lawrence Erlbaum Associates; 1994:17-41.

69. Downs E, Smith SL. Keeping Abreast of Hypersexuality: A Video Game Character Content Analysis. *Sex Roles*. 2010;62:721-733.

70. Dill K, Brown BP, Collins MA. Effects of exposure to sex-stereotyped video game characters on tolerance of sexual harassment. *Sex Roles*. 2008;44:1402-1408.

71. Stermer SP, Burkley M. SeX-Box: Exposure to Sexist Video Games Predicts Benevolent Sexism. *Psychol Pop Media Cult*. 2012.

72. Breuer J, Kowert R, Festl R, Quandt T. Sexist games=sexist gamers? A longitudinal study on the relationship between video game use and sexist attitudes. *Cyberpsychology, Behav Soc Netw*. 2015;18(4):197-202.

73. Haniver J. Not In The Kitchen Anymore. Available at: *http://www.notinthekitchenanymore.com/*.

74. Fat, Ugly, or Slutty. Available at: *http://fatuglyorslutty.com/*.

75. Matthew E. Sexism in Video Games: There Is Sexism in Gaming. *pricecharting.com*. 2012. Available at: *http://blog.pricecharting.com/2012/09/emilyami-sexism-in-video-games-study.html*.

76. Brehem A. Navigating the feminine in massively multiplayer online games: gender in World of Warcraft. *Front Psychol*. 2013;4:1-12.

77. Kasumovic MM, Kuzenkoff JH. Insights into Sexism: Male Status and Performance Moderates Female-Directed Hostile and Amicable Behaviour. *PLoS One*. 2015;10(7). doi:0.1371/journal.pone.0131613.

78. Lucas K, Sherry J. Sex Differences in Video Game Play: A Communication-Based Explanation. *Communic Res*. 2004;31(5):499-523.

79. Tang WY, Fox J. Men's harassment behavior in online video games: Personality traits and game factors. *Aggress Behav.* 2016. doi:10.1002/ab.21646.

80. Hansen DJ, Christopher JS, Nangle DW. Adolescent heterosocial interactions and dating BT - Handbook of Social Development: A Lifespan Perspective. In: van Hasselt VB, Hersen M, eds. *Handbook of Social Development: A Lifespan Perspective.* New York: Plenum Press; 1992:371-394.

81. Field T, Lang C, Yando R, Bendell D. Adolescents' intimacy with parents and friends. *Adolescence.* 1995;30(117):113-140.

82. Bandura A. Social learning through imitation BT - Nebraska Symposium on Motivation. In: Jones MR, ed. *Nebraska Symposium on Motivation.* Lincoln: University of Nebraska Press; 1962.

83. Bandura A. *Social Foundations of Thought and Action: A Social Cognitive Theory.* Englewood Cliffs: Prentice-Hall; 1986.

84. Cummings HM, Vandewater EA. Relation of adolescent video game play to time spent in other activities. *Arch Pediatr Adolesc Med.* 2007;161(7):689.

85. Kowert R, Domahidi E, Festl R, Quandt T. Social gaming, lonely life? The impact of digital game play on adolescents' social circles. *Comput Human Behav.* 2014. doi:10.1016/j. chb.2014.04.003.

86. Smyth J. Beyond Self-Selection in Video Game Play. *Cyberpsychology Behav.* 2007;10(5):717-721.

87. Williams D. Groups and goblins: The social and civic impact of online games. *J Broadcast Electron Media.* 2006;50:651-681. doi:10.1207/s15506878jobem5004_5.

88. Domahidi E, Festl R, Quandt T. To dwell among gamers: Investigating the relationship between social online game use and gaming-related friendships. *Comput Human Behav.* 2014;35:107-115.

89. Engles R, Dekovic M, Meeus W. Parenting Practices, Social Skills, and Peer Relationships in Adolescence. *Soc Behav Personal.* 2002;30(1):3-17.

90. Moore R, Ducheneaut N, Nickell E. Doing Virtually Nothing: Awareness and Accountability in Massively Multiplayer Online Worlds. *Comput Support Coop Work*. 2007;16(3):265-305.

91. Naumann L, Vazire S, Rentfrow P, Gosling S. Personality Judgments Based on Physical Appearance. *Personal Soc Psychol Bull*. 2009;(35):1661-1671.

92. Kowert R. *Video Games and Social Competence*. New York: Routledge; 2015.

93. Kowert R, Domahidi E, Quandt T. The Relationship Between Online Video Game Involvement and Gaming-Related Friendships Among Emotionally Sensitive Individuals. *Cyberpsychology, Behav Soc Netw*. 2014. doi:10.1089/cyber.2013.0656.

94. Kowert R, Vogelgesang J, Festl R, Quandt T. Psychosocial causes and consequences of online video game involvement. *Comput Human Behav*. 2015;45:51-58. doi:10.1016/j.chb.2014.11.074.

95. Lemmens J, Valkenburg P, Peter J. Psychological causes and consequences of pathological gaming. *Comput Human Behav*. 2011;27(1):144-152. doi:10.1016/j.chb.2010.07.015.

96. Liu M, Peng W. Cognitive and psychological predictors of the negative outcomes associated with playing MMOGs (massively multiplayer online games). *Comput Human Behav*. 2009;25(6):1306-1311. doi:10.1016/j.chb.2009.06.002.

97. Roberts LD, Smith L, Pollock C. "U r a lot bolder on the net": shyness and Internet use BT - *Shyness, development, consolidation, and change. In: Shyness, Development, Consolidation, and Change*. New York: Routledge; 2000:121-135.

98. Yuen CN, Lavin MJ. Internet Dependence in the Collegiate Population: The Role of Shyness. *Cyberpsychology Behav*. 2004;7(4):379-383.

99. Valkenburg P, Schouten AP, Peter J. Adolescents' identity experiments on the internet. *New Media Soc*. 2005;7(3):383-402.

100. Kowert R, Oldmeadow JA. The Stereotype of Online Gamers: New Characterization or Recycled Prototype. In: *Nordic DiGRA: Games in Culture and Society Conference Proceedings*. *Tampere, Finland: DiGRA*; 2012.

101. Senlow G. Playing videogames: the electronic friend. *J Commun.* 1984;34(2):148-156.

102. Sherry JL. Flow and Media Enjoyment. *Commun Theory.* 2004;14:328-347. doi:10.1093/ct/14.4.328.

103. Bowman ND, Kowert R, Ferguson CJ. The impact of video game play on human (and orc) creativity. In: Green GP, Kaufman JC, eds. *Video Games and Creativity.* San Diego: Academic Press; 2015:43-58.

104. Mengel F. Computer games and prosocial behaviour. *PLoS One.* 2014;9(4).

105. Lu L, Shen C, Williams D. Friending your way up the ladder: Connecting massive multiplayer online game behaviors with offline leadership. *Comput Human Behav.* 2014;35:54-60.

106. Chiang O. How playing videogames can boost your career. *cbc.ca.* 2010. Available at: *http://www.cbc.ca/technology/story/2010/07/21/f-forbes-videogames-career-leadership.html.*

Made in the USA
Lexington, KY
08 December 2017